A GOOGOLPLEX OF MICE

MIKE PEARCE

DEDICATION

This story is dedicated to all those who love or hate mice
especially in enormous numbers.

CONTENTS

ACKNOWLEDGMENTS

The author would like to thank Christine Pearce
for reading and checking through the manuscript.

PREFACE

You've probably seen films on pest control where hundreds of mice are found living in a barn. The pest controller lifts up a board and out they scuttle in all directions. Well this story is about mice, more than one could ever imagine or count that take over a village and cause chaos.

1 DISCOVERY

It all happened very suddenly. A young girl, Sally Winkle was walking one day along the banks of the canal. The water looked very dark and murky. In places one could see an old supermarket trolley sticking up surrounded by floating plastic bottles and pieces of wood. The sun was shining brightly through the trees. Sally gazed towards the town and saw the ploughed fields ready for planting cauliflowers which grew huge in the fields because of the chalky soil. One field looked bright white. She thought it was covered in chalk which is often brought up by ploughing. Sally had never seen soil that bright before. Sally decided that on her way she would walk through the field. There were two sparrow hawks hovering over it. Sally climbed over the stile and saw that the surface of the field was actually moving in a circular motion. To her amazement the ground was teeming with thousands upon thousands of little white mice which moved quickly to the side like water in front of an oncoming boat. Sally thought that she must inform someone as this could be a large problem if they reached the town. One female could produce hundreds of offspring and with all these mice that's an enormous problem. There were houses that backed onto this field. Sally went down the alley between them and looked over the garden walls, and their backyards were also covered in mice scuttling to and fro. Sally could see in one of the sheds a heaving mass, several layers thick, scrambling over each other like a plague of locusts.

This definitely was a plague of mice. There's not much to eat on a bare field for mice desperate to get food. Possibly bits of left over cauliflower but this was not popular and also remains of corn harvests if it had not all been eaten by birds. The wind blew across the field ruffling their fur first in one direction then the other. The mice seemed to avoid Sally and did not go near to her. It would be no use the farmer planting seeds this year. They would just be eaten straight away she thought. The bags of seed would also be bitten through.

She continued through the alley, it was heaving with

mice all going in one direction. The walls either side of the alley were used like a small racetrack, mice competing to pass each other on the top of the wall and some falling off in the process. She reached the end of the alley where mice were branching off in different directions. It was peculiar how distinct groups did not mingle together but kept apart from one another. Sally thought that each group must all be the descendants from families. Some of the mice looked very old, some had lost part of their ears, some were partially blind, while others had lost part if not all of their tails or bits of fur possibly from fighting.

Sally knew that one female could have at least ten litters a year with twelve or more mice per litter. This was a googolplex of mice, uncountable. In amongst this ocean of white mice Sally knew there could be great, great, great, great, great, great, great, great, great, great, great, great, great, great, great grandmothers and grandfathers, plus, husbands, wives, fathers mothers, sons and daughters, brothers and sisters, aunts and uncles, cousins, nephews, nieces, mothers in laws, fathers in law, brothers in law, sisters in law etc. etc. all feeding and breeding together.

2 GRANDMOTHERS

Just over the road at the end of the alley was her grandmother's cottage. Sally was carrying a basket of food as she knew some foods would not be delivered by the delivery vans. The food in the basket had not been attacked by mice as the basket had a strong plastic cover over it. She reached the door of the cottage. She knew the key was always kept under the door mat. She picked it up and opened the door and several mice ran inside. She thought, oh dear, but could see the house was already full of mice. She called out and heard a faint cry from the back room. Her gran was sitting in her rocking chair. Sally said, "How you? Ok? There's mice everywhere."

"Mice," she said. "I haven't seen one for years." Her eyesight was very poor, and Sally could see mice even looking through her spectacles left on the side table.

"Are you warm at night?"

"Fine," she said. "I've got my hot water bottle and a

lovely warm furry blanket." The furry blanket Sally saw was a sheet of sleeping mice. Sally looked over at the dresser in the room. Mice were nesting inside cups and jugs hanging there.

"I'll make you a cup of tea," she said. "I've brought some in my basket." She went to the cupboard to see if there were any biscuits but there was nothing, all biscuits, packets and cereals had been devastated. She opened the fridge and found it full of dead mice standing erect like soldiers in a line. They had run inside and froze to death. She threw them out into the bin. The milk inside had gone off, so she took some powdered milk in a tin from the cupboard and added some to the tea. She went over to her gran and saw that her lap was full of mice but when they saw her they scuttled off. She gave her the tea and she took out some chocolate chip biscuits from her basket but had to flick off two mice that were trying to eat through the bottom of the basket. She put the basket inside the fridge to protect it from these scavengers.

"Where's your cat?" Sally said.

"It's dead," she said. There were so many mice to eat it didn't want any food. Sally knew it must have overgorged itself on mice and died.

The television was on. The set was an old one and the mice liked to sit on the top. Behind the television the mice had formed a big heap wedged between the wall and the back. It was warm there which is why there were so many together. Sally could see mice running along the picture rails along the top of hanging pictures and jumping onto the curtains. Sally went to pull the curtains fully back, but she couldn't as there were so many mice hanging on them it weighed a ton.

"When did you last vacuum this place?" said Sally.

"Vacuum not working," gran said.

"Let me look at it." Sally switched it on, but nothing was sucking. She switched it off and on several times, then shook the end like a whip when suddenly a mouse flew out of the end of the pipe right across the room. Then it started to suck. Sally gave the room a quick vacuum, the best she could, trying to avoid mice on the carpet.

Her gran lived downstairs mainly in this one room where the bed was. She said it saved heating the whole house. She had not been upstairs for years.

"It must be very dusty up there," she said.

"Do go and have a look dear while you're here. There may have been some leaks from the roof or a burst pipe or something. Please have a look"

Sally slowly went upstairs. Mice ran out of her way as she ascended holding the thick mahogany banister tightly as she went up in case the mice tripped her up. On the landing was a very tall china vase which had held dried bull rushes. The big black heads were no longer on show, removed by the mice and just twelve thin stalks now stood up in the pot. Sally reached the top of the landing. Here the wall paper had become faded and browner and pieces were peeling off in places. She pushed open one of the doors to what was previously the bedroom There were piles of clothes everywhere on the bed, floor and inside the wardrobes. Sally could see lots of little nests formed by the mice in them. She lifted up a woolly jumper and several baby pinkies fell down onto the floor. Cobwebs covered all the corners of the rooms and the windows, the net curtains had rotted, and the curtains also were beginning to rot. She looked at the bottom of the wardrobe. There were lots of beautiful golden shoes there. Sally picked one up and out jumped a mouse, then another, and another. She looked underneath the shoe. There was a hole right through the base and mice were using it as a tunnel.

She then went into the bathroom. The sink and the bath were full of mice, many scrabbling up the sides but falling back. She could see that under these mice were piles of dead ones who, like these, were never able to climb out. The smell was horrendous and mouse droppings were everywhere. The upper floors were the mouse highways, streams of mice running from room to room squeaking as they went. Sally left the rooms and did not dare go into the loft as she knew there would be hundreds of mice up there and if she lifted up the hatch they may all come tumbling down on top of her. She could hear mice running around up there, and she had heard them in the chimney in the room. She slowly went down the stairs and piles of mice ran down after her like water from a water fall. Many landed in heaps at the foot of the stairs then ran off. She decided that it was no longer safe for her gran to be in the cottage with hundreds of mice and decided to ring her parents to bring her home to safety for a while. They were most concerned and agreed. Gran struggled to put on her gloves, but it was difficult as mice had made a nest inside them

3 TRIP THROUGH TOWN

She put on her gran's shoes coat and hat after removing mice hiding in the pockets of her coat. The wheelchair, thank goodness, was still intact. She lifted her up out of her chair and walked her to the hall and put her into the wheel chair. She pushed her towards the front door crushing lots of mice as she went. She opened the front door and in plunged hundreds more mice. Sally ran in kicking the mice out of the way as she made her way to the fridge to retrieve her basket. It was her favourite one that her mother had given her and mice had already started chewing it. Outside the pavements and the whole street was seething with mice. They ran out of the way when Sally approached. If they didn't they were soon squashed under the wheelchair's wheels. Like the mice people were scurrying in all directions. It didn't do to hang around for long chatting as the mice would climb up you and sit on anything they could balance on. Many people were walking around with at least half a dozen mice on their heads. If you brushed them off, another six would soon replace therm. When it rained people opening up umbrellas would get a shower of mice on their heads.

The plague of mice had several days ago reached the town. Shoppers by now had learnt that they had to compete with mice for food. The baker had solved the problem by putting his cooked bread in huge tin barrels which the mice could not penetrate. Food in the freezer shops was also safe as long as the sliding glass lids were not left open. Also, tinned food such as soups, canned meat and vegetables were all safe. When shoppers walked around the supermarkets mice would jump through the holes in their trolleys, and if allowed to remain there, start biting into packets or eating vegetables. Mice also had the habit of climbing up inside men's trousers and under women's skirts and every now and then one could hear women screaming for someone to remove them. Vegetables were safe in fridges or fridge cabinets. Mice did not seem to like raw meat, so butchers could carry on as normal. At the till the cashier had to quickly speed up her conveyer belt and the shopper pack her goods into mouse proof bags. Cashiers had large, long fly swatter like sticks to whack any mice that tried to jump on the food on the belt. One could see that mice had sometimes tried to jump into the tills but had been trapped when the till drawer had been shut. On the floor underneath was a pile of mice heads and tails of these unfortunate creatures. It was the same in the hairdresser or salons. There were lots of tails and even heads lying on the floor amongst the cut off pieces of hair. Those who had run in front of the scissors and shavers had met their fate. It was impossible now to eat out as mice would be on your plate before you knew it. Sachets of sauces had holes in them as mice had attempted to chew off the ends and crawl inside. This meant that mice were scurrying around covered in bright red ketchup which people thought was blood which came from them attacking humans.

In the fish and chip shops they had started serving battered mice. Originally meant for cats but now people seemed to enjoy this delicacy, bones and all. The mice were first exposed to a bare flame to burn off their hair before being battered and fried with the fish and chips. Many mice just fell into the oil and the fish and chip owner fished them out with a net and in the flame the hair really burnt off brightly. Many thought they were delicious and crunchy. Others thought this disgusting. It was not a first. Egyptians had fed mice to people who were ill and in World War 2 creamed mice were popular for some people.

Sally did not dare eat such mice; she preferred chocolate bars covered in batter. She carried on pushing her gran through the town past the shops. She could see lines of dead mice squashed in the roads from cars and lorries. But these were soon covered up by more mice. Drivers put their hands to their ears as they started their cars as trapped mice in the exhaust would be shot out with a tremendous bang which shook terrier cars. It was no use depending on cats to catch the mice; they were all in a frenzy, fed up with the taste of them. Dogs ignored them, and many had mice riding along on the dog's backs. As they passed the hospital gran said while they were moving that she had had a letter from the hospital for a blood test. She pulled out the letter from her bag and gave it to Sally. Sally read it and the appointment was today, so she decided to push her in to have the test while they were passing. It was a huge building, there were crowds of people queuing outside and it was difficult to get to the door. Mice were all over the place. People were angry and trying to stand on them as they stood there. "Why are you so angry?" Sally asked.

"We've been bitten," they said. The doctor has said that we should have tetanus injections. Many people have died from sepsis, so they were desperate." Sally went into the blood section of the hospital. She could see into the wards as they passed by. Mice were everywhere even in the patients beds and some were standing up on top of them shouting. Nurses were doing their best to keep them calm, but it was very difficult. In the operating theatre they had huge, fine netting from wall to ceiling so that mice could not enter.

4 ATTEMPTS FOR CONTROL

Fine netting was now being sold in shops, often trimmed with elastic around the edge, so that it could fit around different objects. Many people were now wearing netted head gear like bee keepers, but the pests involved were much bigger and did not sting. Cat nets were sold out for protecting babies in prams or pushchairs as well as mosquito nets.

 The council had already taken some measures. Road sweepers were sweeping mice up in their hundreds with extra-large brushes then picking them up with their shovels and tossing them into their bins which now contained a solution of strong formalin. Roadside bins were stuffed full of dead mice and even dog litter bins. Dog poo was now deposited under the bins on the floor which was beginning to really smell. Road cleaning machines were adapted for sweeping up mice venturing into the gutters. They all tried to get out once inside. Huge snow ploughs were also pushing mice into large piles which were lifted up and dropped into lorries containing formalin solution.

However much they tried, the mice still kept coming.

A few pest controllers were about putting on what was a really pathetic attempt of stalling the onslaught. They were dressed for the job in white coveralls with hoods like those used in sterile conditions or handling radioactive substances. Several held garden flame throwers used to burn off weeds. They also had modified tasers and electric rods to kill off groups of mice, although many mice were just stunned and lay twitching on the ground upside down. Some shops had already set up electric barriers, but these were not foolproof. Leaf blowers were modified for sucking up mice and did quite well except when too many were sucked up at a time and blocked the blower. The men had to point them up into the air and shoot them out like a fountain. One man had brought into town a team of lively foxhounds which were not much good at catching mice but could quickly help change the direction of flow that the mice were running. Electronic ultrasonic transmitters were also becoming common. Many shops and houses were installing them, to protect merchandise as they were supposed to deter mice, but as there were so many they got used to the sound.

Novelty ideas also came to the front. Children were given grabbers for getting hold of mice and fishing nets which had a button where they could turn on a current and electrocute them.

There were also sticky trap paths that children could put down outside their houses so that if the mice ran across them they would be stuck, roll over and get even more stuck Best of all were the adapted mousetraps, small castles and garages had doors for mice to enter and they would drop down inside and be trapped. Pressing a button would cause a metal bar to come down on them like a normal mouse trap. Even darts and small bows and arrows were in demand as well as pellet guns.

 Poisons were put down but as the mice bred so much they soon became resistant and unfortunately other animals such as dogs ate the poisons and died. Excessive use was now restricted. When Sally went into town she saw examples of these but was most intrigued to see old gentlemen sitting on benches, walls or even the tops of buildings fishing for mice, using pieces of cheese as bait. In swimming pools mice could swim in swarms across one side to the other. Pool attendants used fine nets to scoop them out, and then threw them into the boilers which heated the pools. In schools there was chaos, children kept their feet off the floor and all were given large rulers to hit away any mice that came near. Many text books were ruined by mice eating them, but the children had never liked them. Small children found that if they chased hundreds of mice into a corner they would form a ball and become entangled with their tails. Once formed, this ball was used as a football. They also found that if they rolled this ball along a street covered in mice the ball would increase in size rather like rolling a snowball. The ball was then much too large to kick but they would roll them down hills. Council workers would come along and collect these balls and drop them into the formalin inside lorries. Children dared not pick up the small balls to throw them like snow balls as they knew they would be bitten by mice struggling to get out. The council had also put out a bounty for killing mice. This was called the Gertrude initiative based on Saint Gertrude, the patron saint of mice. Unfortunately, often people would hand in just the tails and there would be many mice still running around without their tails. There were so many mice that even the council ran out of money.

5 ARRIVAL AT HOME

Sally at last was past the town. Her gran was happy to be away from it all. Sally lived with her parents on a hill surrounded by rivers which acted as barriers to the mice. She hustled her gran inside her parents' house and checked that no mice were carried in on their persons. It only needed one male and female then they would be in trouble. Though, if they had brought in mice they would soon be dispatched as the house was right next to a wood full of owls, hawks and crows and the river had many herons. Several mice had tried to reach the house by climbing at night upside down along telephone wires, but they had been caught by barn owls.

Sally's parents greeted Sally's gran and settled her down into their spare room which was very cosy with not a mouse in sight. That evening they were due to go and listen to a concert just on the edge of town, but gran decided to stay home. It was eight o'clock; the concert would start at 8.30. It was quiet, and Sally thought the mice must be sleeping in this area. Many mice were known to move onto people's roofs at night and come down in the day which was unusual as mice were known to be more active at night. They arrived at the hall it was only small. People were gradually drifting in to take their seats. It was still quiet, not a mouse in sight. All the people were now sitting down, and the orchestra had been set up and the conductor was ready. The lights dimmed, and the orchestra started up. But something was wrong; some instruments didn't seem to be working.

The brass section were blowing their hardest but no sounds were coming out until all together, like people being fired out of a cannon, a rain of mice showered down on the audience. Mice had been nesting in their instruments. At the same time strings on violins and cellos broke and flew off as did strings on the harp. They had been chewed through by mice.

It is said that a similar thing happened to the Assyrians' bows in 686BC so that they lost the battle. The battle was certainly lost here, and the noise had woken up hundreds of mice from beneath the stage which rushed out into the audience making them flee to the door. The concert was cancelled and people went home disappointed.

6 EVERYDAY MICE

From their home on the hill Sally and her family could see the field and the top of houses covered in mice and numbers increasing as the days went by. Much of the town was in darkness; the mice had chewed through electric cables, a way of keeping their teeth from growing too long.

There had been severe weather for the last few days and mice in the town had become very inactive and breeding had temporarily stopped.

People in the town in time had got used to the mice and the mice seemed to fit in with the people's routines. They knew when they were not wanted. People lived with them. They ate with them, played with them and prayed with them. Children were also getting used to the mice involving them with their toys and games. Mice would be put in and sit quietly in trucks in children's railways, remote control cars and boats. They would be put on slides or play in tunnels and ball pits. They ran through tunnels, were put into the holes in shape sorters, and even put in toy ovens but never cooked. Mice loved birthdays as they would tunnel into birthday cakes and poke their little heads out at the sides. Some mice would burrow right up to the top through the icing to eat chocolate buttons. They had to take care, especially when the candles were lit, which could easily burn off their whiskers. The effect of mice was especially bad, particularly for the elderly. Many were starving.

Any ecologist will tell you that when numbers of animals or humans get extremely high in a restricted area there is always a disaster. Either the numbers of animals preying on them will increase or disease or lack of food will make the numbers tumble to lower levels. There is often violence from males and Sally could see that the numbers of mice were declining. Winter was coming and this year it was an extremely cold one, dropping to below -10 with wind-chill. Mice inside the houses survived but outside they were frozen to death. There was less discarded food so less energy for raising litters. Sally walked into town. Dead mice were everywhere; some sheltered in doorways but would soon succumb to the cold. The council were sweeping them up in their millions; many were taken to a digester to be used for fuel. Sally went back to her gran's house. There had been no heating and no food available for months. A few mice ran around in front of her, but the rest had died or moved out. Sally had brought two cats with her so that her gran could be free of mice when she returned.

7 NOT OVER YET

Crops were returning to the fields. Good harvests were the order of the day, rainfall was plentiful and the days were sunny. Sally decided to visit her gran again, who had moved back home in a few months ago. She walked along the canal. A local group had tidied it up and no rubbish was floating or lying in the canal any longer. She looked over the fields and could see no mice. She reached the end of the alley. Again it was clear of mice, also in the gardens either side. She got half way and looked behind her. A ton of mice several feet high were rapidly racing, scrambling towards her. The mice were back. They must have been in the fields but hidden under the cauliflowers which was not their favourite food.

She took the key from under the mat. At her gran's she opened the door to be met by two very fat cats. It was horrendous, the hall and the stairs were full, nearly as high as the ceiling with writhing mice. She pulled up her hood and held it tight over her face and plunged her way through this great wall of mice. She reached the door of the back room but had difficulty opening it. She pushed hard, and it opened slightly as the mound of mice toppled over. She thought of disaster as with all these mice her gran would certainly be dead. The door opened slowly a bit more, then a bit more. She peered inside, there was her gran sitting still in her rocking chair rocking to and fro as happy as a lark. She was singing and shaking a large pan held over her cooker range. Sally approached her and looked into the pan. It was full of wriggling mice in fat. She saw Sally and said, "Join me for dinner/ best meals I've had for years." She'd been eating mice for breakfast, dinner and tea and looked healthier than she'd ever been. Sally drew back as her gran lifted one of the mice cooked in oil up in the air by its tail and dropped into it into her open mouth. The mice were back, but this time it was as if a deep river had flooded the town. Mice numbers were waist high and very hungry.

"Oh, for another chilly winter," Sally shouted, and headed back to her house, a river of mice following her every step of the way.

To see other publications below by the author visit
snappysnappybooks.com

<u>The really, really, really useful series</u>

How to be a Successful Business Weed
How to Deal with Life's Snakes and Ladders
Know Your Students and Build Your Image
Pens for Pops
How to be a Successful Charity Shop
Make up-revealed
Ronnie's Sermon snippets
Wastefulness-Bone and Urine
Fertility Stones and Chocolate Eggs
Clingers, creepers and scramblers
I Herring Gull
Viking Bay-Natural History

<u>Other books by Mike Pearce:</u>

Pattern for Purpose- God's and Man's designs
Red Fred Cell and Friends
Human Termites eat London
Pigeons Splat London
Glass Anemones Tentacle-ize London
Tuppeny Hangover
I am Termite
The littlest Oyster
Bits and Bobs
The Shell Man
Cats at Christmas
Tails, Tales
Trust-Nothing but a Must
In a Dark, Dark Corner was the Holy Ghost
The Shell Lady
Captain Grottbuster versus the Grey World

London's Nemesis (Trilogy of 3, 4 and 5 above
Saved by Angels (Trilogy of 6, 8 and 14 above)
The World of Wax
Photosynthetic Women
Queen Rat on Deadman's Island
The Watcher on the Fal
The Rock Pool
The Little Shepherd Boy's Gift
The Living Fossils
Old Mother Nature Laughed and Laughed
Betty's Barcodes
Time Runs Dry (play)
Valentines Cards
The Scrofula Infirmary
The Cornish Urchin
My Therizinosaurus
Spider in the Tomb
The White Cockerel
The Red Church Doll
Butterfly Angels (compilation of previous books)
The Girl Under the Paeony Tree
Baby Feet
The Sparrows' Last Soul
Ball Rooms
Absorbed by a Woman
St Mildred-Patron Saint of Thanet
The Slothful Wife
The Tuppeny Bear
The Boy who found Christmas
Nothing but leaves
The Giant's Toothpick
The Night Mare
The Old Pot and the Golden Shoes
Sitting next to Angels

Exodus to a leaf
The forlorn fruit fly
The Pawnbroker's Souls
The Nursery Rhyme Cat
A Call Under the Sea
Dead Donkey Lane

ABOUT THE AUTHOR

Dr Mike Pearce is a scientist interested in behaviour. He also was a lecturer in human biology and health at a college in Canterbury, Kent

www.ingramcontent.com/pod-product-compliance
Lightning Source LLC
Chambersburg PA
CBHW051926250726
48659CB00002B/870